Mr. Monday, The Ice Cream Man:
A Story for Young Economists Seeking to Understand Monopolies

by Lee Weldon Bailiff

~ 2 ~

Published in the United States of America by Lee Weldon Bailiff

ISBN: 978-0-9857917-2-8

Dedicated to
my sons

Mr. Monday, The Ice Cream Man:
A Story for Young Economists
Seeking to Understand Monopolies

Part One

The children of Happy Woods enjoyed the summer months. They did not have to go to school. Carefree play, running, jumping, and bicycle riding filled their days. They also got ice cream every week. Each Friday afternoon, the song would begin playing. First, the children could just barely make out the whisper of notes on the still air. But, the sound of the song always grew louder and louder as Mr. Monday's ice cream truck drew nearer.

The shouts of joy echoed throughout Happy Woods and the parents smiled - each remembering buying ice cream from the ice cream man when they were children.

Before leaving their homes to play on Fridays, the children made sure to ask their parents for the three shiny quarters it would take for them to get an ice cream cone. No one worried about Mr. Monday running out of cones. He always came to Happy Woods well prepared.

Mr. Monday loved Happy Woods. It was the neighborhood with the most children - and the most parents who didn't mind spending seventy-five cents per week on ice cream. He was able to earn a nice living in Happy Woods and his life was comfortable.

...

One week, Mr. Monday made a surprising discovery - a discovery that troubled him greatly. Another ice cream salesman had discovered Happy Woods. Mr. Jolly arrived on Thursday, with a wider variety of treats than Mr. Monday. Mr. Jolly sold each treat for seventy cents. The parents liked Mr. Jolly. He wore a bright smile and his shouts of 'Good afternoon!' were so full of joy. The children befriended him immediately and he told jokes as they crowded around his truck, handing over the coins and taking their treats. Mr. Monday only made two sales that Friday - to the Falstaff twins who had been to the doctor and missed Mr. Jolly's truck the day before. They asked Mr. Monday why his ice cream was more expensive than Mr. Jolly's ice cream. Mr. Monday sold two cones for a total of $1.40. He drove slowly home.

...

~ 8 ~

Mr. Monday sat at his kitchen table
drinking a glass of chocolate milk. He sat
and he drank and he thought. He thought
about Mr. Jolly. How was Mr. Jolly able to
make money by selling his ice cream at
lower prices than he was? If Mr. Monday
dropped his prices so that they were the
same as Mr. Jolly, he'd hardly make
anything at all. The money he made from
selling ice cream had to pay for gasoline, for
fixing the truck when it broke down, for all
the new ice cream cones and cartons of ice
cream, and for all of his bills. Mr. Monday
sold ice cream in a different neighborhood
each day, but Friday was the day he made
the most money, so Happy Woods was very
important to him. What was he going to do
about this new problem? What was he
going to do about Mr. Jolly?

Before he went to bed that evening, Mr.
Monday had come up with an idea. He had
figured out a way to get rid of Mr. Jolly and

get everything in Happy Woods back to normal. He fell asleep with a smile on his face.

Thinking Questions for Part One

1. Why did Mr. Monday like selling ice cream in Happy Woods?

2. Why was Mr. Monday upset when Mr. Jolly came to Happy Woods and started selling ice cream, too?

3. Why did the Falstaff twins pay a total of $1.40 for their ice cream cones when Mr. Monday charged $0.75 per cone?

4. Why didn't Mr. Monday want to lower his prices so that they were the same as Mr. Jolly's prices?

5. Talk with your parents about what you think Mr. Monday should do.

Part Two

The next week arrived and the children were very, very excited. They had just learned the most amazing news from Mr. Monday. All of his ice creams were thirty-five cents each! They could all buy two ice creams for the price of one of Mr. Jolly's ice cream treats! There was giggling and jumping and lots and lots of ice cream. Everyone smiled and shouted "Thank you!" loud and clear at Mr. Monday.

Mr. Jolly stood at the sales window of his truck, leaning on his elbows, watching the children with so much delicious ice cream. Mr. Jolly stood there looking very, very thoughtful. He realized he would sell no ice cream today. In fact, he realized he would never sell another cone or treat in Happy Woods ever again. There was no way Mr. Jolly could ever drop his price to thirty-five cents per treat. He would lose money.

~ 11 ~

Mr. Jolly loved selling ice cream to children, but he could only afford to do so if the children could afford to pay him enough so that he could then pay everyone that gave him what he needed.

He was thinking about his bills and his costs just as Mr. Monday had thought about his bills and his costs last Friday.

Mr. Jolly gave the distant children one more smile, breathed a sigh of resignation, and drove away.

...

Mr. Monday smiled wide. He won. He beat Mr. Jolly at his own game. Happy Woods was his again.

He had sold twice as many cones and treats as usual. But, each one he sold caused him to lose money. He had to dig into his savings account to fund this experiment.

Thankfully, it was successful. He did not have enough savings to do something like this for very long.

He would have to raise his prices next week to make up for all the money he had lost today and last week. The children would be upset. Well, actually, it seemed more likely that their parents would be upset. But, Mr. Monday could tell each child that more discount surprises would be in store in the future ... sometime. He couldn't give any specifics because he certainly couldn't afford any discounts for a long time. But, open-ended promises created hope and hope for a more affordable future would help his customers take it easy on him right now when his prices needed to be higher than ever before.

...

As expected, the children looked confused when Mr. Monday told them that each ice cream cone or treat would cost $1.50. Their parents were convinced the children were playing a trick on them, so they gave out no extra money. Most of the children pooled their resources and shared the treats they purchased. No cones were bought - only treats the children felt they could easily divide.

Mr. Monday was slightly concerned. He had expected that fewer treats would be bought at these higher prices, but he admitted to himself that he was unprepared for such a drastic drop in the number of total treats purchased.

Not only that, but Tommy Swanson had refused to buy any treats at all. He turned on his red and chrome bicycle and rode away.

...

Little did Mr. Monday know, but Tommy Swanson was going to Pleasant Pines. He had learned from his cousin, who lived in Pleasant Pines, that Mr. Jolly was selling ice creams there today.

Mr. Jolly was surprised to see Tommy Swanson at his truck. He asked him why he wanted to pay seventy cents for a treat that he could get from Mr. Monday for thirty-five cents. Tommy told Mr. Jolly everything that was happening in Happy Woods.

Mr. Jolly leaned on his elbows and looked very confused. Why would Mr. Monday have such very low prices one week, and then have such very high prices the next week? Mr. Jolly told Tommy that it was too late for him to change his schedule that day, but that once next week came around, he would be selling his treats in Happy Woods for seventy cents each.

Tommy Swanson ate his chocolate mint delight ice cream cone with a larger than usual smile on his sticky young face.

...

Mr. Monday was very upset. Once more, all of the children of Happy Woods crowded around Mr. Jolly's truck, handing over seventy cents per ice cream treat. No one missed the ice cream this week because of a doctor's appointment - not even the Falstaff twins. Mr. Monday did not sell a single treat. He would have to take drastic measures. He would have to make Mr. Jolly know that there was no way to keep up with him. He would lower his prices like he did before. This time, he would lower them even more. And, he would tell the children he was keeping his promise. See? There are discounts that come in the future! But, this time, he would tell the children that they would only get more discounts if they didn't buy ice cream treats from any other person.

Yes. That was the way to prevent Mr. Jolly from ever coming back.

Mr. Monday drove his ice cream truck away from Happy Woods and tried to make some money in Pleasant Pines. The children of Pleasant Pines weren't permitted by their parents to buy nearly as much ice cream as the children of Happy Woods, so he only sold a few treats at $1.50 each. Mr. Monday had a lot of catching up to do if he was going to stop losing money.

Thinking he had things under control and that everything would be back to normal soon enough, he went to sleep that night and only tossed and turned a little bit.

Thinking Questions for Part Two

1. Why did Mr. Jolly have to leave Happy Woods without selling any ice creams at the beginning of Part Two?

2. How come Mr. Monday was able to sell his ice creams for such a low price?

3. Was Mr. Monday making any money?

4. How did Mr. Monday think he was going to make everything better once Mr. Jolly left and he didn't have to worry about Mr. Jolly's pricing anymore?

5. Why did Tommy Swanson ride his bicycle to Pleasant Pines?

6. Why did Mr. Jolly know he could return to Happy Woods and sell his ice creams there?

7. Talk with your parents about what you think Mr. Monday should do.

8. Talk with your parents about what you think Mr. Jolly should do.

Part Three

Twenty-five cents per treat. Each child purchased three treats. Their dinners were most likely ruined, but how could they turn down such an opportunity? Mr. Monday had kept his promise about future discounts. They had all quickly forgiven him for the high prices he charged last week. This was simply too good a gift. Not one child could think of a reason to hold any grudges against Mr. Monday.

All the children wondered why Mr. Monday insisted that they would only get future discounts if they bought ice cream from him and not from any other seller. They weren't worried about next week. They were all too busy enjoying the twenty-five cent treats.

Just as he had done two Fridays ago, Mr. Jolly stood at the sales window of his truck and leaned on his elbows, thinking. What was Mr. Monday up to? There was no way he could afford to charge such low prices. Why would Mr. Monday choose to lose money just to keep him from selling ice cream? He shook his head in confusion and drove his truck to Pleasant Pines.

Mr. Monday was very excited when he saw Mr. Jolly drive away.

...

Mr. Monday had never seen so many puzzled faces before. Their initial smiles had vanished so very quickly. The children simply didn't understand why they had to pay $2.00 per ice cream treat. A few muttered that they really didn't feel like eating any ice cream this week.

He reminded the children that if they continued to buy ice cream from him, they would be able to receive discounts in the future. They didn't seem to care.

Tommy Swanson turned away on his bicycle and rode off without so much as a good-bye.

~ 21 ~

After twenty minutes and passionate pleading, Mr. Monday thought he was about to convince some of the children to pool their resources and purchase some ice cream. Then the unthinkable happened. Mr. Jolly arrived.

Mr. Monday didn't see when it happened. He just looked up one moment and Mr. Jolly was down the block. Tommy Swanson was already purchasing ice cream from him. All the children fled from Mr. Monday's expensive treats to Mr. Jolly.

How did Mr. Jolly find out? How did Mr. Jolly find out that his prices had changed? Mr. Monday just didn't understand how everything could have gone so very wrong.

It was hopeless. Mr. Monday had simply lost too much money over the past few weeks. He would have to sell his truck and his supplies and find another job.

The next week, the children were surprised to see that the only truck in the neighborhood belonged to Mr. Jolly. Where was Mr. Monday? They wondered about it for a very short while and then crowded around Mr. Jolly's window, shouting out requests. Mr. Jolly told wonderful jokes and they all laughed and ate their treats. Mr. Jolly had good ice cream.

They soon forgot all about Mr. Monday.

Thinking Questions for Part Three

1. Why did Mr. Monday lower his price so much at the beginning of Part Three?

2. What happened the last time Mr. Monday lowered his price a lot (in Part Two) and why?

3. Did the same thing that happened in Part Two happen in Part Three? Why, or why not?

4. Why did Mr. Monday have to sell his truck and his supplies at the end of Part Three?

5. Why did the children soon forget about Mr. Monday?

Part Four

All of the parents of Happy Woods went to the elementary school auditorium to cast their ballots. It was voting day and the Town needed a new Council and a new Mayor. As the parents looked down their ballots, smiles appeared when their eyes read "Mr. Monday" as one of the possible Town Council selections. They all thought it was wonderful that the old ice cream man was running for a spot on the Town Council. They all voted for him.

When the ballots were all counted, Mr. Monday had won a seat on the Town Council. In his victory speech, Mr. Monday talked about solving the horrible problem of competition. He said that the Town didn't need to be torn apart by people seeking to be better than other people. Mr. Monday assured his audience that what made the Town truly great was the sense of togetherness and community every neighborhood had with the others. He explained to everyone that he planned on starting at the most basic level: the sale of ice cream treats to children.

...

Mr. Jolly looked in his mailbox and saw a very important-looking letter. The envelope had a clear window in the front covered with a thin layer of plastic. His name and address were typed out in a bold font and there were big, red words written above his name and address: **Important! Do not discard. Immediate response required!**

He opened the letter and read:

"Dear Mr. Jolly,

According to the new Town Ordinance #1131, you are required to obtain a license for the sale and distribution of ice cream treats. Only one license-holder may conduct business within each neighborhood. Your designated neighborhood is Pleasant Pines. You may not sell ice cream treats in any other neighborhood. If you violate Town Ordinance #1131, your license will be forfeit and you will no longer be able to legally sell ice cream treats in this Town.

Please immediately fill out the enclosed form acknowledging your receipt and understanding of this notice.

Sincerely,

Mr. Monday
Town Councilmember
Chairman of the Committee for Fair Exchange"

Mr. Jolly was very upset. He drove his ice cream truck through many neighborhoods during the week. Now he was required to only go to one neighborhood. He would have to take a second job in order to pay his bills. He might even have to raise his prices a little bit. He did not like the fact that this would make it harder for some of the children to buy his treats. But, his options were limited. His costs had been forced higher by this new limit on the number of his customers.

He silently filled out the enclosed form and placed it in the mailbox for the next day's pick-up.

Thinking Questions for Part Four

1. Why did the parents all vote for Mr. Monday?

2. What new rule did Mr. Monday want to enforce?

3. Why did Mr. Monday want this new rule?

4. What does Mr. Jolly have to do now? Can he still sell ice cream wherever he wants?

5. Do you think the children of Happy Woods will be happy with this new rule? If so, why? If not, why not?

6. Do you think the parents of Happy Woods will be happy with this new rule? If so, why? If not, why not?

7. What do you think Mr. Monday is going to do next? Why?

Part Five

Tommy Swanson noticed first. Mr. Monday's truck was back in their neighborhood, and all of his ice cream treats were $2.00.

He could not find Mr. Jolly in Happy Woods. Tommy decided to ride his bicycle to Pleasant Pines in search of more affordable ice cream treats, but not before telling the others.

Mr. Monday watched in silence as the children all rode their bikes away from Happy Woods. He could not believe his bad luck. He had forgotten that the children could still choose to go where the ice cream was more affordable. He sat in his truck and shook his head.

There was only one thing to do. He would have to get another ordinance passed. It was the only way to guarantee that the market would finally be fair.

...

The parents of Happy Woods each received an important-looking letter in their mailboxes. Big, red words were written above their names and addresses: Important! Do not discard. Monitoring begins immediately!

The letter read:

"Dear Concerned Parent,

According to the new Town Ordinance #1132, all children who wish to purchase ice cream treats may only do so in the neighborhood of their residence. In an effort to maintain fair access to ice cream treats and a fair market for the merchants of these treats, it is necessary to require the children to remain in their own neighborhoods and dedicate their business to their own ice cream seller.

In order to guarantee that Town Ordinance #1132 is adequately observed, each neighborhood will have a monitor posted to it. This monitor has the authority to issue citations to all violators prohibiting access to ice cream treats. Fines may be issued to repeat offenders.

Please direct all inquiries to the Town Council Public Relations Secretary.

Your compliance and continued patronage of your friendly, neighborhood ice cream seller is appreciated.

Sincerely,

Mr. Monday
Town Councilmember
Chairman of the Committee for Fair Exchange"

The parents were all very bothered by this turn of events. The parents felt their children should be free to ride their bicycles where they wanted and spend their allowances on whatever ice cream treats they wanted - no matter where the seller was.

The parents of Happy Woods began calling each other.

The parents of Pleasant Pines began calling each other.

The parents of each and every neighborhood in the Town began calling each other.

Meetings were scheduled and discussions took place.

The next day, parents were walking around the entire Town taking signatures for a petition to have another election for the Town Council.

By the end of the day, everyone had signed it.

...

The Mayor looked perplexed. A petition with the signatures of every parent of every child in the Town sat on his desk. A new election was now required according to

Town Ordinance #13. He hoped he had not upset anyone.

...

All of the parents of the Town crowded into a number of elementary school auditoriums to vote in the emergency election. They all wore smiles and greeted each other joyfully. The children played on the playgrounds as the parents talked and voted. At the end of the day, all of the ballots for the emergency election sat in boxes waiting to be counted.

...

The Ex-Mayor looked perplexed. He had been voted out of office. Everyone had been voted out of office. The entire Town Council had been replaced with parents. Mr. Sunny from Happy Woods was now the Mayor. What had he done? He simply could not think of a single thing said or done which could have upset so many parents. He packed up his desk and started thinking about applying for a job. Perhaps, he thought, he could sell ice cream. He had always enjoyed ice cream, and everyone liked the ice cream man, didn't they?

Thinking Questions for Part Five

1. Why did the children all go to Pleasant Pines at the beginning of Part Five?

2. How did Mr. Monday respond to the children all leaving Happy Woods for Pleasant Pines?

3. How did the parents respond to the new Town Ordinance #1132?

4. Why do you think the parents of the Town voted out all of the Town Councilmembers and the Mayor?

5. Why do you think they voted for other parents to take the places of all the Town Councilmembers and the Mayor?

6. What do you think is going to happen to Town Ordinances #1131 and #1132? Why?

Part Six

Tommy Swanson saw him first. Mr. Jolly laughed and greeted him warmly as Tommy stopped his bicycle right in front of Mr. Jolly's ice cream truck.

There he was. Mr. Jolly. In his same old truck, selling the same old ice cream treats at the same old prices. All the children laughed and played. Everyone felt satisfied. Everyone felt like they got their money's worth.

The new Mayor, Mr. Sunny, had worked with the new Town Councilmembers to repeal Town Ordinance #1131 and Town Ordinance #1132. Now, anyone who wanted to sell ice cream could do so wherever he wished to do so. Now, any child from any neighborhood could go to any other neighborhood and buy ice cream treats from any ice cream seller he wanted to.

Everyone was happy.

Everyone except for Mr. Monday.

Mr. Monday sat on a bench in the park at the center of Happy Woods.

Tommy Swanson rode his bike up to Mr. Monday and asked him what the matter was.

Mr. Monday explained to Thomas how he could no longer sell ice cream because he could not compete with the prices charged by Mr. Jolly. All he wanted to do was make money by selling ice cream. It simply wasn't fair that he could not do that.

Tommy looked sympathetically at Mr. Monday and said he was sorry.

Before riding off to join his friends, he looked up at him at said, "Sir, life isn't fair. Some of my friends run faster than me and some of my friends jump higher than me. It isn't fair. But, I'm better at riding a bicycle than any of them are. And, that isn't fair either. You need to find something to do that you do better than other people. That won't be fair. But, it will be an unfairness that makes you money and that seems better than an unfairness that loses you money. Goodbye, Sir."

Mr. Monday just sat there, still and silent. He thought long and hard. Eventually, Mr. Monday stood up from the bench, walked to his truck, and drove home.

Upon entering his house, he greeted his wife with a hug and a kiss and asked her a simple question.

"Honey?" he inquired. "What do you think I'm good at? Really, really good at?"

Mrs. Monday looked lovingly at her husband and smiled.

"That's easy, dear," she replied. "You can fix anything."

~ 41 ~

"Then, that's what I'll do, I suppose," Mr. Monday agreed.

"I'll start fixing things."

Thinking Questions for Part Six

1. What happened after Mr. Sunny and the Town Council repealed Town Ordinance #1131 and Town Ordnance #1132? Why?

2. Was everyone happy with the results? Why, or why not?

3. What was Mr. Monday worried about? Why?

4. Is Mr. Monday ever going to be able to have a job again? Explain why or why not.

Explanatory Note To Parents

Many consider monopolies to be inherently bad things. They fear that a company with 'monopoly power' will 'fleece the consumer' by charging 'outrageous prices' that the consumers will be forced to pay if they want the good or service provided by the monopolist. This story you have read with your children is my attempt to explain why these fears are unnecessary so long as the market is free.

Bureaucrats within the Department of Justice look for companies that charge prices they consider to be 'below market prices.' They assume that such prices are efforts by those companies to drive competitors out of business so they can then experience 'monopoly power.' The companies in question must then attempt to prove their innocence to the Department of Justice. The bureaucrats never explain how they are somehow able to determine what market prices should be better than those companies and investors who are actually participating in those markets.

As seen in the story, there are some fundamental problems with this concept. If companies do, indeed, choose to price their merchandise below the cost of providing that merchandise, then those companies are choosing to lose money. If these companies choose to lose money right now in order to drive out all competitors and then raise their prices once these competitors are all out of business, they are going to create an incentive for more businesses to enter those markets.

Businesses exist to make money. They make money by providing things people want at prices people are willing to pay. The more efficiently a business is able to do this, the more profitable that business will be. So, it

~ 44 ~

makes perfect sense for more and more businesses to want to provide goods or services the higher and higher the prices for those goods and services get.

The only way a business can have a monopoly (a complete absence of competitors) in a free market is to provide a good or service to the consumer absolutely better than anyone else can. This means, that company will have to provide that good or service for a price lower than any other business can offer. This is very, very, very rare. Also, the great fortunes of modern American industry were not built by selling things to consumers at high prices, but by selling them at low prices.

Henry Ford lowered the cost of an automobile to the average citizen. But, Henry Ford also had competitors. Sam Walton lowered the cost of groceries, clothing, and household items to the average citizen. But, Sam Walton also had competitors.

For a company to charge high prices and experience no competition, the government must be involved as a barrier to entry for any potential competitor. If government obstructions are removed, history has shown us that more gets produced and sold at lower prices than before, and economics has explained to us the reasons why.

In fact, the term 'monopoly' used to only ever be applied to those producers who had received an explicit, special privilege from the party in power - be it king, queen or emperor.. This special privilege, when combined with the power the crown held over which companies were permitted to form in the first place, effectively shielded the favored producer from any threat of competition. It is no wonder that consumers, since centuries past, would thus view the monopolist with disdain.

It is remarkably curious to see how, over the centuries, those with political power created such an evil emotional attachment to the word 'monopoly' by directly interfering in the market, only to eventually turn around and attempt to apply that term to producers engaging freely in the marketplace, all to justify further state interference and control.

Autobiographical Note

I have been teaching undergraduate economic principles since 2006 and possess a bachelor's and a master's degree in economics from Baylor University. I have taught at Tarrant County College and Texas Christian University. I have always enjoyed economics and the role economic thought plays in making all kinds of complicated topics more sensible. Economics is, at heart, the study of the most efficient allocation of scarce resources - resources which have a number of potential uses. In a nutshell, it all boils down to efficiency. The more efficient the allocation of scarce resources, the more wealthy the society, and the higher the average standard of life experienced by the members of that society.

This is important material to understand. Children receive very little instruction in economic thinking. I want to change that.

This book, as well as the others I am publishing in this series, will be useful for any parent that wants to help his or her children understand basic economic principles. I am taking core concepts and filtering them down to their most fundamental level. I hope that the stories I tell entertain as well as challenge the child's mind. It's never too early to exercise the thinking muscle.

While it is true that these books are written primarily with the homeschooling of my own children in mind, they are perfectly suited to children in any educational atmosphere. All that is really required is a parent that wants his or her child to learn about economics.

Thank you for reading.

- LWB

www.ingramcontent.com/pod-product-compliance
Lightning Source LLC
Chambersburg PA
CBHW041717200326
41520CB00001B/143